THE Amazing Animal RESCUE TEAM

Written by Rebecca Blankenhorn
Illustrated by Éva Vágréti Cockrille

STECK-VAUGHN COMPANY

A Division of Harcourt Brace & Company

www.steck-vaughn.com

CONTENTS

CHAPTER 1
Waiting for an Assignment

*I*t was a bright day in June when three members of the World Animal Rescue Team were waiting in their clubhouse for their newest assignment. Last summer they had helped with many animal rescues.

"What are you reading about, Charla?" asked Scott.

"Tigers," said Charla. "Did you know that there are only 5,000 tigers left in the wild?"

"No," said Scott. "Has your brother Michael ever rescued a tiger?"

"Oh, yes," said Charla. "After Michael graduated from college, his first job as a veterinarian for the World Animal Rescue Team was helping to airlift a tiger and her cubs to a safety zone for endangered wildlife in India."

"Cool," said Ray. "I hope we get to help a tiger some day."

"Remember going to Africa, when Michael fixed a cheetah's broken leg?" asked Ray.

"Poor thing," said Charla. "The world's fastest land mammal limped around for weeks."

"But when he got better, he was sprinting at nearly 70 miles per hour!" said Scott.

"I wonder what our new assignment will be," said Ray.

"Yeah," said Scott. "I can't wait to see Michael this summer."

Suddenly, the computer beeped and blinked. It was signaling that new e-mail had arrived.

"This could be it!" said Ray.

"Who is it from?" asked Scott.

"It's from my brother, Michael," said Charla. "He has a new assignment for us."

TO: Charla, Scott, and Ray

FROM: Michael @ World Animal Rescue Team Headquarters

ASSIGNMENT: In Australia, hundreds of wallabies have invaded a small town. They are trying to escape a brush fire. We need to help round up the wallabies and move them to a nature preserve until the fire is out. I'll pick you up in two hours.

CHAPTER 2
Wallaby Roundup

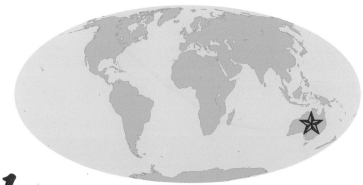

*L*ater that day, the World Animal Rescue Team was on an airplane about to take off for Australia. Charla, Ray, and Scott had lots of questions for Michael.

Scott asked, "How can it be early summer here but late autumn in Australia?"

"Australia is a continent on the southern part of the earth," said Michael. "There the seasons of the year are the opposite of what we have here."

"So when it is winter here, people in Australia are enjoying summer," said Ray.

"That's right," said Michael. "Here, let's take a look at the map and find Australia."

"Can you tell us more about the wallabies?" asked Charla.

"Sure," said Michael. "This is a photo of a wallaby. There are many different kinds of wallabies. They are about the size of a dog. But some wallabies are about the size of a rabbit. The wallabies we will be working with are about three feet long from head to tail and weigh about 35 pounds."

"It looks like a little kangaroo," said Charla.

"Yes, it is very similar," said Michael. "Wallabies are marsupials like kangaroos. The mothers raise their babies in a pouch on their tummies. Baby wallabies and baby kangaroos are called joeys."

"Do they hop like kangaroos?" asked Scott.

"You bet!" said Michael. "They are quick hoppers. Usually these wallabies stay out in the wild away from people."

"What do they eat?" asked Ray.

"Wallabies eat grass and other plants, just like kangaroos," said Michael.

"Now, they're probably bouncing around people's yards and lawns looking for food," said Charla.

"Could be," said Michael. "I'm sure they will be much happier once we get them to the nature preserve. An Australian ranger named Nigel will take us to the town where the wallabies are."

When the World Animal Rescue Team arrived at the airport, Nigel was there to pick them up. Everyone loaded into his truck, and Nigel hurried toward town. Once they arrived, they had to drive slowly because wallabies were hopping in the streets.

"Wow!" said Scott. "How are we ever going to catch them?"

"Let me tell you, mate, we can't catch each one by hand. It will be easier to herd them together and load them into trucks for the ride to the nature preserve."

"Let's get started," said Michael. "Nigel and I will put a tall fence around this park and playground. You three can start rounding up wallabies."

"It will take us forever to get all those wallabies into the park," said Ray. "Won't we need more help?"

"Don't worry," said Nigel. "The people who live here will help us. The police will stop traffic, so the streets will be clear. Just wave your arms and shout. Then walk behind a wallaby and guide it in the right direction."

"Everybody, check your watches and get your walkie-talkies and compasses. Keep in touch every ten minutes. This park will be our base. Scott, you start out going west. Charla, you go south. Ray, you go east," said Michael.

"Too bad we don't have horses," said Scott. "This is kind of like a rodeo!"

Later, Charla got on her walkie-talkie and asked, "Scott, how many wallabies have you brought in from the west?"

"I've rounded up about ten so far," said Scott. "Have you seen Ray?"

"Not yet," said Charla. "Why don't you call him?"

"Good idea," said Scott. He held his walkie-talkie and called, "Come in, Ray. Over."

Ray's voice came through loud and clear on the walkie-talkie, "This is Ray. Over."

"Where are you?" asked Scott. "The wallaby pen is getting really full. We're almost done. Over."

"I'm bringing in one more right now. Wait for me at the base. Over," said Ray.

Ray's last wallaby was giving him quite a chase. First it darted across three backyards and then it hopped over some bushes. When Ray caught up to it, the wallaby was eating grass.

"I've got you," whispered Ray. But the wallaby moved away from Ray. Then it stopped, realizing it was trapped. Ray took another step toward it, and this time the wallaby took a big hop toward Ray, then another one, and another one!

Uh-oh, thought Ray. It's coming right at me! "Hold on there, little wallaby. Stop!" shouted Ray. The wallaby kept coming and with one powerful leap jumped over Ray's head and bounded away.

Ray followed the wallaby until he caught it. Then he met the rest of the team.

"That roundup was a workout," said Ray.

"Well, you all did a great job," said Michael.

"What happens now?" asked Charla.

"As long as the fire is burning, these wallabies will have to stay at the nature preserve. When the fire is out, they will be taken back to their homes. But now, our job is done," said Michael.

Just as they were getting into the truck, Michael's laptop computer blinked. He checked his e-mail and told the team, "We have another assignment!"

TO: Michael and team

FROM: World Animal Rescue Team Headquarters

ASSIGNMENT: A baby aye-aye is stuck in a tree in Madagascar. Report to the airport as soon as possible. Your guide, Anna, will meet you once you arrive.

CHAPTER 3
Aye-aye Aye!

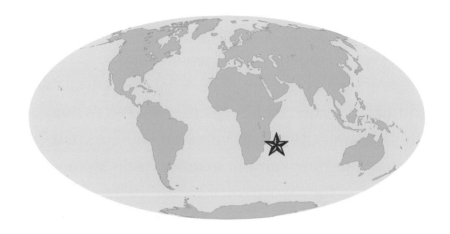

*A*t the airport, Scott asked Michael, "Where is Madagascar?"

Michael said, "Madagascar is a small island country on the east coast of Africa. It is warm and humid there. On the northern side of the island there are mountains. On the southern side of the island there are deserts. The eastern side of Madagascar has forests. That's exactly where we will be going next. Here, let's find Madagascar on my map."

"How do you say the animal's name?" asked Charla.

"Its name sounds like the word *I*," said Michael.

"That name reminds me of a joke," said Scott. "Knock, knock."

"Who's there?" asked Charla and Ray.

"Aye-aye," said Scott.

"Aye-aye who?" asked Charla and Ray.

"Aye-aye, ear ear, foot foot," said Scott.

"Oh, that is so silly," laughed Ray.

"I wonder how an aye-aye looks," said Charla.

"Here's a picture of one," said Michael.

"Yikes!" said Ray. "Look at those huge eyes!"

Michael told them, "The aye-aye is about the size of a house cat. It is a primate like a monkey. It is most active at night. Its large eyes help it to see. It eats bugs that it picks out of trees with its fingers."

After a long airplane ride, the World Animal Rescue Team arrived in Madagascar. Their guide, Anna, was waiting for them. Everyone loaded into her van and drove to the rain forest. There, it was steamy, lush, and green. Chameleons and insects peered down at them from the trees. The whole forest seemed to buzz. Everyone followed Anna as she led them through the forest.

"We don't often see aye-ayes in the daytime," said Anna. "So it was quite a surprise to find a mother and her baby out in the open. Then I realized that the baby was stuck in the tree."

"The baby must have been reaching for bugs and gotten its arms full of sticky sap," said Michael.

Anna said, "We'll have to use a large net to hold the mother while we get the baby out of the tree."

As they approached a clearing,
Anna told the team to stay very quiet.
"It's just a little further," she whispered.
"Follow me."

Then they stopped and saw the baby
aye-aye struggling on the tree.

"It's scared," said Charla. "We have to help it."

"How will we get it down?" whispered Ray.

"We will have to use our tree-climbing
equipment," said Michael.

Michael put on his tree-climbing equipment.
Anna got the large net ready. Then she crept up
behind the mother aye-aye and caught her.

"Charla, you and I will climb up and get the baby," said Michael.

Charla put on her tree-climbing equipment. She gulped as she started climbing, one foot at a time, up to the crying baby aye-aye.

On the ground, the mother aye-aye was screeching under the net, but Anna held on to it tightly. High up in the tree, Michael and Charla were still climbing. Finally, they reached the baby aye-aye, who was quite cranky from being stuck for so long. Michael quickly squirted vegetable oil on its little arms to help get it out of the tree.

"It's hard to get a grip with these gloves on," said Charla, as she carefully loosened the baby's pointy fingers.

"I think it's working," said Michael, as he gently pulled the baby's arms free.

"We did it!" said Charla. She passed the squirming, sticky, furry creature to Michael and said, "Now we can get down!"

Ray put on rubber gloves to help clean the baby. Michael held it, while Scott and Ray wiped it off.

"We're getting really goopy," said Ray.

Anna called, "Hey, you guys, the mother really wants to go to her baby. Are you almost done?"

"The baby aye-aye is about as clean as it can get. We only need to measure it. Then we can carry it to those trees and let it go," said Michael.

"Why do we need to measure it?" asked Scott.

Michael told him, "When a new baby aye-aye is discovered, we need to make sure it is healthy and growing strong. It won't take long."

"We're done, Anna," shouted Charla.

They released the baby, and it scampered to a tree. Then Anna set the mother free. The mother aye-aye raced to its baby. She scooped the baby up and carried it up the tree.

Charla said, "Whew! I hope the baby aye-aye doesn't get stuck again."

Anna said, "Hopefully, that baby aye-aye will learn to choose better trees for hunting insects."

Scott, Ray, and Charla began packing up the equipment.

"You all were amazing! That was a great rescue," said Michael as he packed.

Then everyone piled into the van for the ride out of the rain forest. Michael took out his laptop computer and checked his e-mail.

"Hold on guys," he said. "I've got another message. It looks like we're on our way again."

TO: Michael and team

FROM: World Animal Rescue Team Headquarters

ASSIGNMENT: Report to Borneo in Indonesia as soon as possible. Injured pangolin needs your help. Ranger Rani will pick you up from the airport.

CHAPTER 4

Pangolin in Trouble

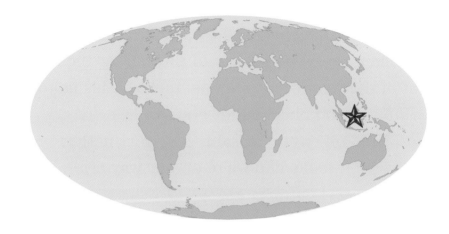

After Michael and the team landed in Borneo, they had to wait for their guide.

"Where are we exactly?" asked Scott.

"What's it going to be like here?" asked Ray.

"Well, Borneo is an island in the western Pacific. Actually, it is the third largest island in the world. It is about 400 miles east of Singapore in the East Indies. It is very warm, steamy, and wet. Some parts of Borneo are rain forests. Let's find Borneo on my map," said Michael.

"Michael, can you tell us more about the pangolin?" asked Ray.

"Sure. It is a scaly anteater that lives in Africa and Asia. Here's a picture," said Michael.

"It's like a pine cone with a tail!" said Scott.

"What are its scales made of?" asked Charla.

"The scales are part of its skin, and the edges are very sharp," said Michael. "The pangolin has no teeth, but it has strong, sharp claws for digging out ant piles and termite mounds."

"How does it eat the ants?" asked Ray.

"Pangolins have very long, sticky tongues that they use to lick up lots of ants," said Michael.

Finally, Ranger Rani came. He drove the team to Ganung Palung National Park, which was more like a jungle than a park. During the ride into the dense rain forest, Rani explained what had happened.

"I was checking on an orangutan in the forest, when I heard something snuffling and digging. I looked carefully and saw a pangolin with a broken foot trying to dig up a termite mound."

"Couldn't you catch the pangolin and help it?" asked Ray.

"Pangolins have a very good defense system," said Rani. "They roll into a tight ball so that only their sharp, scaly skin is showing. It's almost impossible for one person to catch a pangolin."

"This is the end of the road," said Rani. "We walk from here."

"Let's put on our backpacks," said Michael.

Rani led them through the forest for a few miles. Their packs felt heavier than ever.

When they stopped to take a rest, Scott said to Charla, "How are we ever going to find one pine cone with legs in this huge jungle?"

Charla smiled and said, "Well, at least there aren't any pine trees out here, so if you see a pine cone, you know it must be a pangolin."

Ray said, "Rani seems to know every inch of this forest. I think we'll be able to find it."

Rani told them, "OK, this is the spot where I last saw the pangolin. Be quiet, because if it senses danger, it will roll up in a ball."

"If it rolls up, then it will look like a brown artichoke," said Michael.

"What's an artichoke?" asked Scott.

"It's a vegetable with scaly and thick leaves. It's shaped like a big rosebud," explained Charla.

Michael told them, "Before we split up, everybody turn on your walkie-talkies."

As they moved through the forest, birds cooed above them. Sometimes monkeys would screech.

Then suddenly Scott heard a scuffling noise behind a tree. He whispered into his walkie-talkie, "Come in, Michael. This is Scott. Something's moving around behind a tree. Over."

Michael's voice came back over the walkie-talkie, "Stay where you are. Over."

Together Michael and Scott stepped closer to the tree. The snorting got louder. They could see dirt flying up from the ground behind the tree. Whatever it was, it was definitely digging!

Just as Michael and Scott looked around the tree, the digging stopped. It was the pangolin. It looked right into their faces and gave a surprised little snort. Then it curled up! Michael called the others over on his walkie-talkie.

"You found it," whispered Charla.

"Good going," said Rani. "We're lucky the pangolin's injured foot is still sticking out."

Michael said, "Now we can treat the pangolin's foot and let it go on its way. First, everyone needs to put on a pair of heavy gloves. Be careful of those sharp scales."

"Will the pangolin have to wear a cast?" asked Scott.

"When I broke my ankle, I had to wear a cast for six weeks, and then the doctor cut it off."

"We will use a special kind of cast," said Michael. "It will last for about a month and then fall apart all by itself so that the pangolin won't have to see a doctor again. Charla, look in my pack to find a splint, some medical tape, and a packet of medical plaster."

Charla and Ray mixed up the plaster. Scott helped Rani tape a splint to the pangolin's foot.

"It sure is a good patient," said Ray. "It doesn't even wiggle."

"We may never know how this pangolin broke its foot," said Rani, "but at least its foot will heal now."

After the pangolin's cast was set, Michael set it down by the tree.

"The pangolin won't uncurl and leave until it thinks we're gone," said Rani.

"Let's move over here and wait," said Michael.

Michael and the rest of the team watched and waited from behind the tree. Then a few minutes later, the pangolin uncurled and scurried away.

"Everyone did great work. What an incredible rescue!" said Michael to the team.

As they were packing up to go, Michael checked his e-mail. "I have some good news," he said. "We get to go curl up in our own homes for a while."

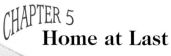

CHAPTER 5
Home at Last

After three weeks of rescues, the World Animal Rescue Team was home. Charla, Ray, and Scott met at the clubhouse to share photos.

"What a great adventure! I liked saving the aye-aye," said Charla, as she showed a photo of the animal. "Look at how long its fingers are. It looks like it should be in a science fiction movie. Sometimes I think it's a cute animal, but it's also kind of creepy looking."

"I wish we could have seen some of the other animals in the rain forests," said Scott.

"When that wallaby leaped over me," said Ray, passing around another snapshot, "I was sure I felt the fur on its belly touching the top of my head. I wonder if Nigel got the wallabies back to their homes."

"I don't know about the wallabies, but I'm glad to be back home for a while," said Scott. "My mom said she saw an armadillo on a camping trip last weekend. Armadillos can roll up in a ball just like a pangolin. I hope the pangolin we helped is feeling better. Say, anyone want to hear a joke?"

"No, thank you!" said Charla and Ray.

AYE-AYE

MADAGASCAR
EAST COAST OF
AFRICA

BORNEO
SOUTHEAST ASIA

PANGOLIN

Then the computer beeped and blinked. "Hurry, check the e-mail," said Scott. "It might be a new assignment."

TO: Charla, Scott, and Ray
FROM: Michael @ World Animal Rescue Team Headquarters
ASSIGNMENT: We're needed in Texas. Mexican free-tailed bats are trapped in an underground cave. Pack your spelunking equipment. I'll pick you up in three hours. We're off again.

"All right!" said Charla, Ray, and Scott together. "It's another amazing rescue for the World Animal Rescue Team."